CONTENTS

Introducing... CAKE!

Can you think of some of the reasons we eat cake? Of course, the main one is that *it's delicious!* But we often eat cake when we are celebrating something too.

In this book, we are going to go on a journey that is all about cake! Along the way, you will find out things about cake that you never knew. You will even get your own cake recipe to try ...

You will also discover when cake was first created and some of the different ways it was made. (The person who invented cake should have won a medal!)

Most cakes are made from butter, sugar, eggs and flour. We're going to take each of these **ingredients** in turn and find out where it comes from and what it does.

This delicious-looking cake has a jam and cream filling. Yum!

Let's start our journey ...

The stages of CAKE

This is how you make a cake like the one in the photo on page 3 ...

Ingredients and tools

You need the following ingredients:

 150 g butter   1 teaspoon vanilla extract

 150 g sugar   150 g plain flour

 3 eggs   2 teaspoons baking powder

You also need a fork (or a whisk, or electric mixer), a bowl and a cake tin.

1 First, mix the butter with the sugar until it forms a paste.

2 Next, add the eggs and vanilla extract and beat until the mixture is smooth.

3 Then, sift in the flour and the baking powder and mix together.

4 Next, add the mixture to the cake tin.

5 Finally, bake it in an oven at 180 °C until it's ready. Ask an adult to help with this.

The science of cake – what does what?

🧁 The sugar makes the cake sweet.

🧁 The vanilla extract helps to improve the flavour.

🧁 The eggs help to bind the mixture together. They also keep the cake moist.

🧁 The **baking powder** has bicarbonate of soda in it. When bicarbonate of soda is added to a liquid (such as eggs), there is a chemical reaction. Bubbles of carbon dioxide gas are formed. The heat from baking also creates carbon dioxide and expands the pockets of air in the mixture. This makes the cake light and fluffy.

🧁 The **gluten** in the flour traps the air bubbles that the baking powder creates. It helps make sure that after the cake rises it doesn't collapse!

Follow that BUTTER!

Cows eat grass, hay and dry feeds, and drink water. The dry feeds are made from **cereals** (not the breakfast kind!) with vitamins and minerals.

Most cows are milked twice a day. Until around 150 years ago, cows were milked by hand.

Moo!

This is where butter starts!

Milking a cow by hand

Look at all those cows!

These days, some of the big dairy farms use massive milking machines. The cows can be milked four or five times a day.

GUESS WHAT?

A Canadian cow named Gillette Emperor Smurf has produced more than 217, 000 litres of milk!

That's over a million small glasses of milk!

The milk is taken to a **creamery**, where a part of the milk called 'cream' is separated out. Then the cream can be made into butter, or into cheese.

Butter used to be made by hand. **Churning** the milk separates it into buttermilk (the liquid part) and butterfat (the solid part). The butterfat is cooled and salt is added so it will stay fresh for longer.

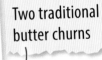

Two traditional butter churns

In some countries, butter is still made the traditional way. This is someone making butter in Namibia.

A creamery makes other products from milk too, such as yoghurt, cream and cheese.

Cream and yoghurt can be made in a day but cheese can take several weeks to make. Some cheeses aren't ready to eat for over a year!

Many kinds of food can be made from milk.

Where SUGAR comes from

Most sugar comes from the sugar cane plant. Sugar cane is grown in **tropical** and **subtropical** areas. Brazil produces more sugar than any other country in the world.

A field of sugar cane

The countries in Europe are cooler. Sugar beets grow well here.

NORTH AMERICA

EUROPE

A

AFRICA

Brazil has a hot, tropical climate that sugar cane grows well in.

SOUTH AMERICA

Sugar beets also give us sugar.

Sugar beets are grown in many countries in Europe. This is because they can be grown in a cooler **climate**.

Sugar is made from the juice of the cane or from **processed** beets.

AUSTRALIA

GUESS WHAT?
Sugar cane is used to make lots of other products too – including fuel for cars!

All green plants produce sugars, but sugar cane and sugar beets produce the highest amounts. The sugar that plants produce is called 'glucose'. Plants use some of the glucose to

grow and then store what they don't need. This stored glucose is **extracted** from the plant. It is then combined with another form of sugar called 'fructose' to make sucrose. Sucrose is the kind of sugar we eat.

Sugar cane must be shredded or crushed before it can be turned into sugar.

A worker feeds sugar cane into a shredding machine.

GUESS WHAT?
To be healthy, we should not eat more than seven spoonfuls of sugar per day – that's less than is found in one can of cola.

Sugar beets being processed in a factory

Sugar beets grow underground. Before they can be made into sugar they need to be washed.

Mud being cleaned off sugar beets

GUESS WHAT?
The tallest cake ever made was 33 metres high. It contained 3370 kg of sugar – that's the same weight as a female elephant!

Chickens and EGGS

Now let's find out where we get the eggs for our cake …

Most of the eggs we eat come from chickens. The eggs you see in the shops usually come from **poultry** farms. Many of these farms are **industrial** farms, which are designed to produce as many eggs as possible. The chickens are kept in cages. This kind of farming is called 'battery-cage' farming and many people think it is cruel to the chickens.

Chickens at a battery-cage farm

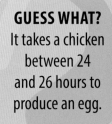

GUESS WHAT?
It takes a chicken between 24 and 26 hours to produce an egg.

Eggs being taken on a conveyor belt to be put in cartons. It would be very messy if they fell!

Another kind of poultry farming is free-range farming. This means the chickens are able to roam about outside. The label on a carton of eggs will tell you if the eggs come from free-range chickens.

Chickens on a free-range farm

There are lots of different **breeds** of chicken. Some lay around 80 eggs a year and others lay up to 320 eggs a year!

cluck!

These are Orpington chickens. This breed of chicken lays around 200 eggs per year.

This chicken is called a Bovan Goldline and is often used in battery farms.

GUESS WHAT?
During the Second World War, fresh eggs were **rationed**, so people had to eat dried eggs instead.

When eggs have been collected, either by hand or by a conveyor belt, they are passed over a strong light to see what is inside. This is called **candling** and makes sure the eggs are of a good quality for eating. The reason it is called candling is that before we had electricity, this was done with a candle.

Follow that FLOUR!

Finally, let's find out where we get the flour to put in the cake …

Most of the flour we use for baking cakes is made from wheat.

Wheat growing in a field

Wheat is grown for both humans and animals to eat. It is sown in the autumn and harvested the following summer.

Before **industrialisation**, harvesting was mostly done by hand, using a tool called a 'scythe'. In some countries, it is still done this way.

Harvesting wheat in Serbia using scythes

Farmers often used horses to help them harvest the wheat more quickly.

A farmer harvesting using horses

These days, many farmers use combine harvesters like this one.

Harvesting wheat in South Africa. This is much faster!

The top of the wheat is called an 'ear'. The grain in the ear of wheat is separated into its various parts: bran, endosperm and germ. It is the endosperm part of the grain that makes flour. It is **ground** until it is a very fine powder (flour).

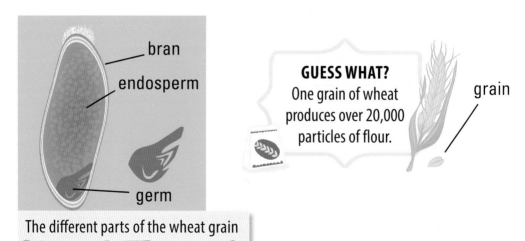

bran

endosperm

germ

The different parts of the wheat grain

GUESS WHAT?
One grain of wheat produces over 20,000 particles of flour.

grain

In early times, flour was ground between two stones. One early method was to grind corn into flour using a mortar and pestle. A mortar is a stone bowl. A pestle is a stone club used to pound the grain.

pestle

mortar

grain

An ancient wheat grinder

Millstones were invented later. Millstones were large disk-shaped stones. The grain was put between two millstones, and then the stones were pushed round and round to crush the grain. People often used waterwheels or windmills to get the power to push the millstones round.

A watermill in Italy

A windmill in the Netherlands

Today, machines are more commonly used to make flour. They crush the wheat between two metal rollers and are usually powered by electricity.

Inside a modern flour mill

GUESS WHAT?
You need around 350 ears of wheat to produce enough flour for a loaf of bread.

In some places such as India, the endosperm of the grain is roughly ground rather than turned into flour. It is then made into flat cakes called 'chapatis'.

A basket of chapatis.

Flour can also be made from other grains such as corn, rye, barley, oat and rice. Often flour has things added to it to make it last longer.

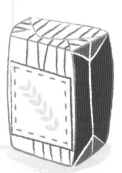

GUESS WHAT?
Did you know that flour can also be made from potatoes, peas, beans and peanuts?

The final DESTINATION

Now we have all the ingredients, they can go to the factory or to your kitchen to be made into cake!

The end of the journey ... almost

The best bit!

Cakes to celebrate

There are lots of different times when we have cake, especially when we're celebrating. Here are some of them. Can you think of any more?

Birthdays

Weddings

Festivals or special times of the year

But wait a minute ... !

I can't eat dairy products like butter and milk.

I can't eat flour because it contains gluten.

I can't eat sugar because I have **diabetes**.

Luckily there are lots of different cake recipes. Some don't have butter, some don't have flour and some don't have sugar!

Make your own CAKE!

Now that you have read all about how cakes are made, why don't you try making your own? Here is our very own banana cake recipe.

Ingredients

 100 g butter

 175 g plain flour

 100 g sugar

 2 teaspoons baking powder

 2 eggs

 2 tablespoons milk

 3 ripe bananas, mashed

 50 g cocoa powder (optional)

1 First, beat the butter and sugar together with a fork, whisk or electric mixer until the mixture is light and fluffy.

2 Then beat in the eggs and bananas.

3 Add the flour and baking powder. (You can add the cocoa powder at this point if you want to make a chocolate-banana cake!)

4 Then add the milk.

5 Mix together well and pour into a greased loaf tin.

6 Finally, bake for 45 minutes at 180 °C. You need to ask an adult to help you because the oven will be hot.

7 Allow to cool, but eat while still warm!

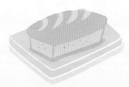

The history of CAKE

800 to 500 BC: The very first cakes were made in Ancient Greece from nuts and honey. They were not light and round – they were flat! They were called *plakos*, which means 'flat'.

800 AD: The word 'cake' came from the Vikings. In their language (Old Norse), the word for cake was *kaka*.

GUESS WHAT?
The reason we say 'a cake of soap' is because of the Vikings. Their cakes were flat and hard, so things that were a similar shape, like soap, were called 'cakes' too.

1700s: In the 1700s, people used 'potash' – potassium carbonate – in cakes. This chemical helped cakes to rise, but it was difficult to make and quite smelly.

1800s: Baking powder began to be added to cakes in the 1800s. This made cakes rise, and made them light and fluffy too.

The end of our journey

'Food miles' is the phrase we use to describe how far food has travelled before it gets to a plate. As you have seen with our cake journey, some ingredients come from a long way away. Using cars, planes and lorries to move food around is not very good for the planet. This is why many people try to eat food that is grown or made locally as much as they can.

The very last journey a cake makes is to our tummies!

Glossary

baking powder   an important baking ingredient that creates a reaction in cake mixture. It makes the cake rise.

breeds   types of animal. For example, Labradors and Poodles are different breeds of dog.

candling   when strong light is passed over an egg to see either if it is of a good quality to be eaten

cereals   different types of grain grown for humans and animals to eat

churning   beating or shaking milk to make butter

climate   the usual weather conditions in an area

creamery   a place where dairy products are made from milk

diabetes   a disease where a person has too much sugar in their blood

extracted   when something useful is taken out of something else

gluten   a protein that is found in cereal grains and different types of flour

ground   to crush a grain to turn it into smaller particles

hard boiled   when an egg has been cooked so it has a firm yolk and is white

industrial   used to describe things made by machines, rather than by hand

industrialisation   when things change from being made by hand to being made by machines

ingredients   the items you need to make something to eat

poultry	the type of birds that are often farmed for their meat and eggs
processed	when something is changed into something else. For instance, milk is processed to make cheese.
rationed	when something is given out in controlled amounts because it is in short supply
subtropical	used to describe areas directly north and south of tropical areas
tropical	used to describe areas and climate near the equator

Index

NOW ANSWER THE QUESTIONS ...

1 What makes cake light and fluffy?

2 What part of milk is used to make butter?

3 Why might cake bakers have been glad when sodium bicarbonate became available?

4 Why do you think the author included a map on p10–11?

5 How many eggs can a chicken lay in a year?

6 How were early cakes different from cakes we like eating today?

7 Why can't some people eat cakes with sugar in them?

8 Which parts of the book did you find most interesting and why?

9 Why do you think the author finished the book with a section on food miles?

10 What is your favourite type of cake? Why do you like it so much?